IDEAS & ISSUES
Intermediate

TEACHER'S GUIDE

Editor Richard Larkham
Designer Valerie Sargent
Cover design Gregor Arthur

GW00585126

Printed in Italy

Teacher's Guide

Ideas & Issues Intermediate (including Grammar Workbook):

Students' Book	ISBN 3-12-508452-0
Teacher's Guide	ISBN 3-12-508453-9
Double Cassette Pack (C1: Reading; C2: Listening)	ISBN 3-12-508432-6
CD Tune in Listening	ISBN 3-12-508459-8

WHAT IS THIS BOOK FOR?

Class discussion is always an attractive option when you are looking for ways to get all your students participating in oral practice. It naturally generates a quantity and flow of language which other activities cannot match. The motivation element is important: unlike so many exercises, discussion gives opportunities to say things you really want to say.

But at the same time, discussion is one of the most difficult exercises to manage successfully. It can drift formlessly, it can be dominated by two or three talkative students, it can end with awkward silences. Part of the problem is that the open-ended nature of the exercise can accentuate the differences in language level among the members of the class. Some students simply lack the language to express their ideas.

Ideas & Issues Intermediate is designed to meet the challenge by providing step-by-step preparation for discussion. The reading and listening texts provide ammunition in language and content. In most cases they give just one side of an argument, which encourages students to agree or disagree strongly and clearly. Ideas start to bounce around the group. The details, the examples and the opinions in the texts provide much more of a stimulus than the simple, bald question often used to launch a discussion.

Ideas & Issues Intermediate is primarily a discussion book; however the 22 authentic reading texts and the 22 listening passages, all with accompanying exercises, are a very useful resource in themselves. There are also writing activities at the end of each unit. So a range of skills other than debate is practised.

HOW TO USE THE BOOK

You do not have to work through from Unit 1 to Unit 22; each one is self-contained and there is no sequence of language level. In fact the units are arranged alphabetically by topic and it is up to you to choose the order in which you use them. It may be that a particular topic is in the news, or it has come up in class because of one student's experience. Or you may want a discussion topic that is specially suitable to practice a language

item. Treat the book as a flexible resource – that is how it has been designed.

Each unit covers four pages – two double-page spreads, the first starting from a reading text, and the second starting from a listening passage. The two spreads are closely related in subject matter but can be treated independently if preferred. Spread 2 widens out the theme of Spread 1 or sometimes approaches it from a different angle. The general structure of each spread is in three parts: the text (reading/listening), language work and then discussion/activities.

Not only can each spread in a unit be used as a free-standing lesson, but also parts of spreads can be isolated and adapted to fit your immediate requirements. You may have no time for a discussion today; but you can still listen to the tape and set a writing exercise for homework.

SPREAD 1

Focus
Rather than going cold into the reading text, you have the chance to focus on the topic with introductory questions. Typically, students are invited to think about their own experiences which may be relevant in the subsequent discussion. At the same time, the aim is to activate useful vocabulary or give an opportunity to pre-teach it.

Read about it
This is the text which will serve as a springboard for discussion. It also provides practice in reading skills. It is followed by a glossary and comprehension questions. These are not just a useful check for the teacher. Answering the questions will often clarify the text and reinforce important new vocabulary. By going through these stages, students approach the point where they can use language and ideas in an effective discussion.

Talk about it
This gives students the opportunity to discuss issues raised by the text, and to go beyond the scope of the text to a wider view. Generally, guidelines for discussion and additional useful vocabulary are offered. Students are sometimes asked for their imaginative input in roleplays. Some of the tasks require writing in advance of

discussion: for example, arranging items on a list in order of importance, or designing a questionnaire.

SPREAD 2

Tune in
As with the reading texts in Spread 1, an introductory question warms up the class by establishing the general topic. It also gives the teacher a chance to check students' language needs; any difficult vocabulary which will occur on the tape can be brought in formally or informally. Note that it will also be helpful to look at the pictures and the other written material on the page before listening to the recordings.

The listening texts are radio discussions, phone-ins and interviews which have been specially written. Naturally, they provide practice in listening skills. But here they have two extra functions: to stimulate students with ideas for the discussion which is to follow, and to equip them with useful language for that discussion. There are questions on the page to check understanding of the listening text.

Key Language
This has the same function as on Spread 1. Sometimes it picks up specifically oral language items, like disagreeing politely or emphasis in speech.

Over to you
This is the final discussion phase of the unit. It covers issues raised by both the written text in Read about it and the listening material in Tune in. Activities include discussion, debate, conducting a survey and roleplay.

Write about it
This provides writing practice for use in class or as homework. Tasks include writing letters and descriptions, and devising a questionnaire.

WORDLISTS

A detailed Wordlist with explanations and definitions begins on page 119. Whereas the Read about it glossary-on-the-page deals with the more difficult and text-specific vocabulary, this wordlist picks up other words with which students might need some help.

Talking Tactics – on the flaps
Certain language functions occur again and again in discussion: **agreeing**, **persuading**, **interrupting** etc. Special flaps on the front and back covers offer a useful selection of the most common of these functions, along with some clear, contextualised examples.

Lesson plan 1

ADVERTISING
This topic is a good one for introducing the book and familiarising your students with the concept of a discussion class in English. People are exposed to advertising every day and all students will have views, whether reactions to particular adverts or more general opinions about the industry.

Focus
[*Timing: 5-7 mins*]
Most students in the class will have opinions about current TV commercials, the latest billboard posters and new, beautiful or shocking magazine advertisements. You may find students want to tell each other in their own language about a "brilliant ad" they recently saw. Make sure you direct classroom exchanges at this stage. Your aim is not only to introduce the topic by getting students to focus on some effective or striking advertisements. It is also important to introduce or activate useful vocabulary such as *ad, TV commercial, product, slogan, promote, portray … as, message, photo, drawing, image, text, words*. Useful phrases for giving reasons for remembering recent advertisements are *I like/hate the music/model/ actor/ product; I see it every day; It's funny/ glamourous/unusual /irritating*.

Read about it
[*Timing: 7-10 mins*]
Although this text will serve as a springboard for discussion later on, use it initially for reading skills practice. First of all, use it for practice in **skimming** (reading to get the general message of the text). Give the students one minute to glance over the text before asking them what it is about.
Then give them practice in **scanning** (reading to find the answer to a specific question). Get them to read the questions in Exercise 2 first. Then give them a minute to re-read the text and find the answers.

Although this book is intended primarily for speaking practice, you may feel your students need a change of pace and activity. If so, get them to write answers to the comprehension questions after/instead of giving them orally.

Finally get students to read the article a third time, more slowly, using the glossary where necessary. It is probably best to avoid asking students to read the text aloud – this is time-consuming and often boring for those who have to listen.

Key Language
[*Timing: 5-10 mins*]
This section will reinforce some of the language your students will need for the discussion later on. Exercise 3 focuses on the modal *might*. Get students to read through the examples showing how it is used. If you think they need to practise some simple transformations before going on to Exercise 3, get them to do a drill like this:

Say the following sentences for the students to change to sentences with *might*.
Perhaps they'll be late. *(They might be late.)*
Perhaps he'll do it. *(He might do it.)*
Perhaps she's wrong. *(She might be wrong.)*
Perhaps there's time. *(There might be time.)*
Perhaps it won't be possible. *(It might not be possible.)*
Perhaps we don't need a new slogan. *(We might not need a new slogan.)*
Perhaps it'll cost too much. *(It might cost too much.)*

Then get your students to transform some *might* sentences to *Perhaps* + future/present. Here are some possible examples:
A photo might work better. *(Perhaps a photo will work better.)*
A poster might be cheaper. *(Perhaps a poster will be cheaper.)*
They might not get the joke. *(Perhaps they won't get the joke.)*
The slogan might be too difficult. *(Perhaps the slogan is too difficult.)*
People might be getting tired of the ad. *(Perhaps people are getting tired of the ad.)*
People might not like the slogan. *(Perhaps people don't/won't like the slogan.)*
Now get students to work through Exercise 3.

Exercise 4 asks students to use some of the words highlighted in the glossary in a new context. Both exercises work equally well as written or oral exercises. If you want to vary the pace and activity, get your students to write the answers after or instead of giving them orally.

Talk about it
[*Timing: 15-20 Mins*]
This is the discussion phase of the lesson and the moment to introduce your students to the Talking Tactics flaps on the front and back covers of the book. Ask the class to spend a few minutes looking at them and explain that they should aim to use a few of these speaking strategies during every discussion.

Divide your class into groups of four to six students. Suggest they appoint one student as chairperson and another as secretary. The chairperson will make sure that everyone gets the chance to express their views. The secretary should make a note of some of the group's opinions. Monitor the groups as they talk, and make a note of the most interesting discussions. At the end, get the secretaries of those groups to report back to the whole class. Questions 5 to 7 are fairly factual and encourage the students to think about the style, content and effectiveness of the Nike advertisement. By analysing the idea and methods behind a single advertisement, the students will be more equipped to give their opinion in the more general Questions 8 and 9. Question 10 offers the most scope for general discussion. Use it either to round off this lesson or as a lead-in to the next double-page spread.

Spread 2 of this unit gives the class fuel for a more general discussion on the rights and wrongs of advertising.

Tune in
Listen to the tape or read the tapescript before the lesson. This will enable you to gauge which new/difficult words you should try to introduce in the warm-up Question 1 before your students start listening.

Question 1 [*Timing: 3 mins*]
Give your students a minute to look at the pictures and think about their answer to Question 1 before you go round the class. On the board write down some of the answers under the headings **Pros and Cons**. Some of the answers they may come up with are:
Pros: *works of art, entertaining, tell you about new products, give you something to look at*

TEACHER'S GUIDE

Cons: *boring, waste of money, increase the cost of products, exploit people, make people spend money they don't have, make people feel bad/jealous/deprived, encourage people to waste money, dishonest.*

Question 2 [*Timing: 3 mins*]
During this first listening students have to listen for the gist of the four opinions. Ask individual students for their answers and, if necessary, add the four opinions to the pros and cons on the board.

Question 3 [*Timing: 3 mins*]
Get the students to read through the sentences to be completed before you play the tape a second time. This phase concentrates on listening for detailed language.

Question 4 [*Timing: 3 mins*]
There are no right or wrong answers here. You might need to give your students a useful shorthand way of referring to each ad when they give their opinions: the Benetton ad, the Chanel No. 5 ad etc.

Question 5 [*Timing: 3 mins*]
Get your students to read through the Talking Tactics phrases for giving and asking opinions before you play the tape a third time.

Question 6 [*Timing: 3 mins*]
This exercise aims to get students trying out some of the key language as they give their opinions. It is not the full discussion phase of the lesson.

Over to you
This is the final discussion phase. Ask your students to spend a few minutes looking at the Talking Tactics flaps. Tell the class to aim to use a few of these speaking strategies during every discussion.

You will not necessarily have time to do all the tasks in this section. Do not feel you should work through all of them. Choose the ones you think will be most stimulating or entertaining. Allocate different exercises to different groups of students and have a feedback session at the end of the lesson when each group reports on the discussion.

For most activities in this phase of the lesson, divide your class into groups of four to six students with a chairperson and a secretary in each. The chairperson should make sure that everyone gets the chance to contribute to the discussion and give their views. The secretary should write notes during the discussion, recording some of the group's opinions.

Monitor the groups as they talk, and make a note of the most interesting discussions. At the end, the secretaries of those groups can report back to the whole class.

Students will find it more stimulating if they change groups for each new discussion. They should not always work with the same people.

Question 7 [*Timing: 5-8 mins*]
Get the whole group to contribute ideas for the one-minute speech and then choose one person to speak to the whole class during final feedback.

Question 8 [*Timing: 5 mins*]
The correct answer is **b**. Students are likely to come up with some jokey slogans as well as serious ones. Encourage them to read out slogans to the rest of the group as they write them; this will generate more creativity.

Question 9 [*Timing: 5-8 mins*]
Students should work in pairs for this activity. Make sure each pair chooses a different product. While not strictly a discussion activity, deciding on the name for the product and dialogue will give students a chance to give opinions.

Question 10 [*Timing: 10 mins*]
This is the activity likely to stimulate the most discussion and disagreement. Encourage the chairperson in each group to put to the vote opinions on the listed ASA rules and make sure each group secretary is recording the results of each discussion.

Write about it
[*Timing: 15-20 mins*]
Set one of these questions for writing practice in class or as homework. Question 11 follows on well from 7, 8 and 9 in Over To You. Question 12 is an ideal follow-up for students who discussed the ASA rules in 10.

Lesson plan 2

DISCIPLINE

This is another good choice for a first discussion class. It is a topic which most teenagers have discussed at home and amongst friends and they will generally have strong views. Spread 1 focuses on discipline at home; Spread 2 looks at discipline at school.

Focus

[*Timing: 5-7 mins*]

Use this part of the lesson to help students feel comfortable about discussing rules at home. Make sure you do not voice your approval or disapproval of the rules they describe! At the same time, try to make students stick to *describing* rules at this stage. They will get an opportunity to criticise them later in the lesson. Use this time to activate useful phrases like *(not) be allowed/ expected/ supposed to, (not) have to, disapprove of, be banned/forbidden, be back by, have friends round.*

Read about it

[*Timing: 5-10 mins*]

Ask the students to read the text silently and answer Question 2. Check their answers. Then ask them to summarise the rules in Becki's and Mark's homes. Students should say a sentence each. Ask the class whether Becki or Mark has more freedom (they'll probably say Mark) and if they can explain it (they may suggest that it's because he's older and a boy). You may decide this is the moment for a discussion on the fairness of different treatment for boys and girls. If so, go on to Talk About It Question 5.

Key Language

[*Timing: 5-10 mins*]

The different ways of talking about rules covered in this section will be useful in the discussion part of the lesson. Point out to students that they don't have to talk about rules that they have to conform to. They can also talk about rules they used to have to obey or which their brothers and sisters have to face. This means all students will be able to take part, whatever their age. This exercise is best done in pairs or small groups. However, after practising it orally, you may feel your students need a change of pace. If so, get them to write a few sentences based on the prompts.

Talk about it

[*Timing: 15-20 mins*]

For this phase of the lesson your students should have the Talking Tactics flaps open. Don't feel you have to work through all the discussion items. Choose the one(s) you want in the order you want – or get different groups to discuss different topics and report on the discussion to the whole class at the end of the lesson. Feel flexible about the timing. It will depend on the interest and concentration of the students whether you want them to spend five or fifteen minutes discussing one topic.

Question 4 Each student could draw up an individual list of family rules before groups compile the list of the five commonest ones. They may then want to find out which are commonest in the other groups. The group chairperson or secretary (see notes to the sample lesson plan for Advertising, Talk About It paragraph 2) will be able to go round the other groups getting that information and passing it on to his/her own group.

Question 5 Make sure the groups include boys and girls (or in single sex schools, students who have a sibling of the opposite sex). At the end of the discussion, if the students need a change of pace, you could ask them to write a summary of the differences and whether the group thinks they are fair.

Question 6 This is probably more suitable for pairwork than in groups. Let students choose the partner they want to work with for this activity.

Question 7 Monitor the groups or pairs as they make their list of rules for parents. In this way, you will be able to choose the groups/pairs with the most thoughtful rules to speak to the class.

Tune in

Listen to the tape or read the tapescript before the lesson.

Question 1 [*Timing: 3 mins*]

Give your students one minute to think of some school rules they know about. Ask a few students to tell the class the ones they have come up with.

Question 2 [*Timing: 3 mins*]

Students should read through Question 2 before you play the tape. You may like to tell them that this is a true story although the names have been changed. During the first listening, students have to listen for the gist of the news story. Get them to write down the letter of the sentence which correctly summarises it: **c.**

Question 3 [*Timing: 5 mins*]

Students should read through the list of events before you play the tape a second time. Read out the answers so they can check their ordering of the events. (See Answer Key)

Questions 4 and 5 [*Timing: 3-5 mins*]

You may not need to play the tape a third time for your class to complete the sentences. Check they have completed the sentences correctly so that in Question 5, they can give the speakers' words in direct speech.

Question 6 [*Timing: 5 mins*]

If you need a change of pace, get your students to write these sentences before they read some of them out.

Over to you

See the Advertising lesson plan, Over to you section on page 6 for some general points on managing this part of the lesson.

Question 7 [*Timing: 5 mins*]

Get students to discuss this topic in groups. They may like to vote within the group for or against the headteacher's expulsion of Sharon and compare their result with the other groups'.

Question 8 [*Timing: 5 mins*]

Monitor the groups as they discuss this topic and encourage the group to reach a consensus. Then have the chairperson of the most original/ thoughtful groups present their conclusions to the rest of the class. As a follow-up to this topic, you may like to set the writing task, Question 11 (Write About It).

Question 9 [*Timing: 5 mins*]

Check that students all agree on the standard punishments given in their school – students often have conflicting ideas on this topic. If students do not have much information about usual types of punishment, they may enjoy playing "judge" and matching what they consider the most appropriate punishments from the list to the commonest "crimes" in the school.

Question 10 [*Timing: 5-10 mins*]

Students can collaborate as they prepare, even though only one student will be able to give the one-minute speech. Choose only willing and confident speakers for this task.

Write about it [*Timing: 15-20 mins*]

Question 11

This can be done in class or as homework. It follows on well from Question 8.

HOW TO USE THE WORKBOOK (pages 96-118)

Each teaching spread in *Ideas & Issues Intermediate* contains a Key Language section which highlights a grammar point, a function or a lexical point from the reading/listening text. These sections consist of a short summary and practise exercises, and are cross-referenced to the Workbook activities at the back of the book. The Workbook section is arranged with one unit to a page. Each starts with an explanation and clear examples of the language point, followed by a variety of exercises.

Some activities provide controlled structural or lexical practise and may be carried out by the students individually or in pairs in class, immediately after they have worked through the Key Language section (e.g. Food, page 14 activities 1 and 2). Or alternatively, they can be used at home as consolidation or revision.

Other activities combine skills (e.g. speaking and writing) and offer freer practise, requiring the students to work in pairs, or in small groups. The written element is usually a follow-up to the discussion, or the result of group consultation (e.g. Honesty, page 17, activity 3).

The Workbook activity types include:

Vocabulary - word search, matching activities, crosswords, gap-fill, jumbled letters, quizzes

Grammar - sentence transformation and inversion, identifying correct usage, matching clauses, sentence correction

Writing - short reports, descriptions, dialogues, lists, questionnaires, informal letters, advertising slogans

Speaking - prediction, acting out a dialogue, reading work aloud, intonation practise, discussion, exchange/comparison of opinion, compiling lists

Answers to the exercises in the Workbook are provided in this Teacher's Guide (pages 15-18).

At the back of the Student's Book:
Pages 119-124: Wordlist
Pages 125-129: Tapescripts of the listening materials (Tune in)

ADVERTISING

(pages 6 & 7)

2 **a** Nike.
  b He has no forearms or legs and he has done the London Marathon.
  c He hopes it will promote disabled sport.
  d Peter likes it because it portrays him as an athlete, not a victim.
  e He's been disabled all his life. He doesn't seem depressed. He seems well-adjusted.

3 **b** A less shocking slogan might give a more positive message.
  c The message might not be very clear.
  d The ad might be exploiting his disability.
  e The ad might shock the public too much.
  f People might say the ad is not in good taste.
  g The ad might offend disabled people.

4 **a** portrays **b** slogan **c** Billboards **d** promote
  e advertising campaign

5 The Nike logo, a tick, is just above the slogan *Just Do It*.

6 Be decisive. Get on with life. Don't waste time. Be courageous.

(pages 8 & 9)

3 **b** " ... the best ads are works of art." **c** " ... too many ads exploit women.' **d** " ... a lot of ads make people feel bad."

8 **b** Worn by Construction Workers since the 1960s.

ANIMAL RIGHTS

(pages 10 & 11)

1 An animal rights activist is someone who takes public action to make sure people treat animals well. They are particularly interested in protecting animals from use in experiments. They take part in demonstrations, hand out leaflets and write to MPs (Members of Parliament).

2 **a** 2.8 million experiments on animals were done in 1994.
  b Growing a human ear on a mouse's back.
  c To find a way of rebuilding ears on people who have lost them or who were born without them.
  d "Obscene", "shocking" and "bizarre".
  e They hope to learn how to treat or cure cancer.

3 **a** The Vacantis hope to help children who are born without ears.
  b They also hope to reconstruct ears which are lost in accidents.
  c Scientists who are experimenting/who experiment with animals get a lot of opposition.
  d Onco-mouse is a rodent which is bred to contract cancer.
  e Animal experiments are essential to scientists who are looking for new medicines.
  f Most animals who live in cages seem unhappy.
  g People shouldn't buy products which are tested on animals.

(pages 12 & 13)

2 Pictures **f** and **c**

3 **a** On horses. **b** Guns. **c** To escape from traps. **d** Rhinos and Siberian tigers. **e** To sell their body parts for use in traditional Chinese medicine.

4 **a** fox-hunting **b** Trapping **c** Wearing **d** Testing **e** Sending **f** Being

ART AND ARTISTS

(pages 14 & 15)

2 Because many people think it is not really art.

3 Animal rights activists are angry about this work. They vandalized (damaged) Hirst's pickled sheep.

4 You would expect the title to mean "a mother divided or separated from her child". In fact, here it means both mother and child cut in half.

5 Perhaps he wants to be famous so that he can increase his prices, or get rich or because he just enjoys public attention.

7 **a** driver **b** guitarist **c** actor **d** author **e** photographer **f** psychiatrist

8 **a** tennis player **b** doctor **c** journalist **d** psychologist **e** teacher **f** skier

(pages 16 & 17)

2 Yes, Tony is proud of what he does and of the art he creates.

3 **a**-A; **b**-A; **c**-D; **d**-D; **e**-D; **f**-A

4 **a** felt tip pen **b** spray cans **c** killed by trains **d** $50,000 for their pictures in a gallery in Manhattan **e** paid **f** enjoy the art that we make

5 **a**+1; **b**+3; **c**+5; **d**+2; **e**+5; **f**+4

BEAUTY

(pages 18 & 19)

The Ugly Duckling, by Hans Christian Andersen, tells the story of a "swan" growing up in a family of ducks. The duck family don't realise the "ugly duckling" is, in fact, a swan. The swan itself only discovers it is a swan when it matures and loses its fluffy grey down and becomes graceful. The phrase "ugly duckling" means a person who is less attractive and less talented than others in the group when young, but who outshines them when older.

3 **a** Because the girl who was having the party thought she was unattractive.
  b Probably because her brother and twin sisters were better-looking and slimmer.
  c They left her out more, stopped inviting her home and drew nasty pictures of her.
  d A boy at the youth club asked her to dance.
  e She tried to improve her appearance by going on a diet, getting contact lenses and growing her hair.

(pages 20 & 21)

2 **b c e f**

3 **a** lip **b** put **c** have **d** stretched **e** have ... put on

BELIEFS

(pages 22 & 23)

2 **f**-1; **d**-2; **h**-3; **g**-4; **i**-5; **a**-6; **e**-7; **c**-8; **b**-9

3 **b** I suggested inviting her home for the weekend. I suggested (that) they should invite her home for the weekend.
  c I suggested not criticising the Moonies. I suggested (that) they shouldn't criticise the Moonies.
  d I suggested not giving her any money. I suggested (that) they didn't give her any money.
  e I suggested finding out more about the cult. I suggested (that) they should find out more about the cult.
  f I suggested going to one of their meetings. I suggested (that) they should go to one of the meetings.

(pages 24 & 25)

2 a-T; b-?; c-T; d-F; e-T; f-T; g-F; h-F; i-F; j-?; k-F; l-T; m-T; n-T; o-T; p-F; q-?

8 If you break a mirror, you'll have seven years of bad luck. It's unlucky to walk under a ladder. You'll have good luck if a black cat "crosses your path" (walks in front of you). Finding a horseshoe is lucky – you have to hang it up with the ends facing upwards so that the luck "can't run out".

CRIME AND PUNISHMENT

(pages 26 & 27)

2 b

3 a **Four** girls were involved in the fight.
b The girls were found guilty of **manslaughter**.
c When they were arrested, they were charged with **murder**.
d Because of good behaviour, their sentence was reduced by **12 months**.
e They will be released just **one year** after the crime.
f The family will put flowers at **Louise's grave**.

4 a released b charge c manslaughter d sentence
e custodial f defence

(pages 28 & 29)

2 He is for the death penalty.

3 32 – men executed so far this year in Texas.
500 – If you take $500 dollars from a shop, you will get maybe two years in prison.
2 – You will get maybe two years in prison.
20 – Killers don't change. They can spend 20 years in prison, and then come out and kill somebody else.
100,000 – It costs almost $100,000 per year to keep a man in prison.

4 a "And, you know, it costs almost $100,000 a year to keep a man in prison. If one of these murderers lives for thirty years, that's $3 million! Do we really want to spend that sort of money on a killer?"
b "These killers don't change. They can spend 20 years in prison and then come out and kill somebody else. If a dog bites you, can ever trust it again?"
c "The Bible says: "An eye for an eye, a tooth for a tooth." If a man kills your daughter, don't you want revenge?"
d "Do they want to live the rest of their lives in prison? Most of them would agree that they'd be better off dead."
e "The death penalty prevents crime. It's the only thing that frightens the killers."

5 1 "If a man kills your daughter, don t you want revenge?"
2 "If a dog bites you, can you ever trust it again?"
3 "Do they want to live the rest of their lives in prison?"
4 "Do we really want to spend that sort of money on a killer?"

6 a Shouldn't we learn from experience?
b Aren't there enough people in prison already?
c Do murderers deserve to live in peace?
d Can we forgive people like this?
e Is this the best way to solve the problem?
f Would you actually do the execution yourself?

DISCIPLINE

(pages 30 & 31)

2 a-T; b-F; c-?; d-T, e-F; f-?

(pages 32 & 33)

2 c

3 h-1; a-2; f-3; i-4; j-5; e-6; b-7; c-8; d-X; g-X; k-X

4 a to remove b to tell c to take it out d to go home
e not to come back

5 (Could you) tell your side of the story. Take it out immediately. Go home. Don't come back to school wearing your nose ring.

DRINK AND DRUGS

(pages 34 & 35)

2 a-F; b-T; c-T; d-F; e-F; f-T

3 a she had started walking b she had learnt to speak quite well
c she had learnt to read d she had finished school
f she had become a university professor

4 (*Suggested answers*) learnt to speak well/started to read/lost some teeth/learnt some simple maths/started learning to swim

(pages 36 & 37)

1 Morphine and similar drugs are used as pain-killers.

2 a He injects it. b He used to smoke it. c He has been taking it for six years.

3 a To be "in" with the young men in his neighbourhood.
b He rejected his parents and teachers (and "that whole generation").
c He had dropped out of school. He didn't have a job.
d He didn't respect himself. He felt bad about himself.

4 a "...when you stop, you feel very, very bad. You get pains everywhere, you vomit, you shiver."
b All his friends are on heroin.
c His daily life revolves around heroin. He says: "When I give up, I don't know how I'm going to, you know, spend my time."

5 Original meaning – a; c
Fillers – b; d; e; f

6 (*Suggested version*) I started smoking when I was, you know, about 13. I mean, lots of kids at school were already smoking by that age. I used to have, you know, a puff of my mum's cigarettes. I mean, she didn't mind. Then I started, you know, buying my own. I mean, in the end I was spending, you know, all my pocket money on cigarettes.

FAMILY

(pages 38 & 39)

1 An arranged marriage is one where the parents choose a husband or wife for their child. This type of marriage is common in Hindu and Moslem cultures.

2 a-F; b-?; c-T; d-F; e-T; f-T

4 a Sarita's father told her that he had found a suitable young man for her.
b He told her that she would definitely like Ranjit.
c He told her that he lived in England.
d He told her that he had a very good job.
e He told her that he was good looking and quite rich.
f He told her that she could meet him later that month.
g He told her that he had arranged a meeting already.

(pages 40 & 41)

2 a With his step-father, who objected to Jim sitting down to dinner without any shoes on.
b Because they were always arguing.

3 a Jim: With his father   **Nadia:** With her mother
b Jim: Two years ago   **Nadia:** Nine years ago
c Jim: His stepfather gets on his nerves   **Nadia:** Finds her father's new wife very bossy
d Jim: *wishes he could see mother on her own*   **Nadia:** Hates her for breaking up the family/Is proud of her sometimes
e Jim: Still very upset   **Nadia:** Relieved

6 a step-father **b** half-sisters **c** remarried
d step-mother; first marriage **e** single parent

FASHION

(pages 42 & 43)

1 a; **d**; **e**; **g**; **h**; **j**

2 a She thinks her figure is worse than it is.
b He thinks being fashionable is more important than it really is.
c She used to be more relaxed about her appearance than now.
d Nowadays young models look unhealthier than they used to.
e Fashion models are thinner than they should be.
f Fashion should be more practical than it is in the fashion magazines.

(pages 44 & 45)

3 a Luke **b** Maria **c** Carl **d** Rose

4 a feminine **b** a snob **c** fashionable **d** different

5 *feel ... like*

6 (*Possible answers*)
a good/comfortable/ attractive
b stylish/fashionable/original?
c original/eccentric/different/well-dressed?
d comfortable ... attractive/fashionable?
e good/best

FILM AND TV

(pages 46 & 47)

2 a videos, television **b** conversation with adults, toys
c They should recognise their names and basic words like "juice" and "bricks".

Key Language
Two other sentences with passive continuous are "The television is be used as a babysitter... " (*paragraph 3*) and "They were not being taught a basic vocabulary through one-to-one conversations with adults" (*paragraph 5*).

3 a are being neglected **b** are not being given
c are being forced **d** are being left **e** is not really being watched **f** are not being taught

4 *Some more examples:*
Many politicians are being criticised about their private lives.
Some students are being given more attention than others.
Old people are being treated badly by society.
I am being paid very little.
Women are being expected to do everything.

(pages 48 & 49)

2 dead; violent; terrible; crimes; shot; killers; murders; violence; copycat

3 a "Society is getting more violent every day. Young people are committing terrible crimes which they didn't dream of committing, say, thirty years ago."
b "After that terrible film *Natural Born Killers* there were a number of "copycat" murders. A teenager in America watched it ten times and then killed his mother and half-sister."
c "The problem is that children can't really tell the difference between fantasy and real violence."
d "Films can cause you to buy certain things or even change your life-style."
e "There are a number of scientific studies, by psychologists, which suggest a link between screen violence and real-life violence."

4 *Possible answers*:
a scream/cry/vomit/faint **c** going to South Africa
d run away with her boyfriend **e** the ones with real human problems in them **f** their teachers or school books

9 The cartoon's serious point is that TV violence is making children behave in a violent way.

FOOD

(pages 50 & 51)

2 a Most teenagers stop eating meat because they are concerned about animals.
b At rock concerts, some animal-rights groups show videos of the worst slaughterhouses.
c Most parents are worried that their children will not get enough protein if they are vegetarians.
d Teenagers say there is a poor selection of vegetarian food in their school cafeteria.
e Giving up meat can sometimes be a warning of an eating disorder.
f Linda Ahkami cooks vegetarian food for her two daughters and non-vegetarian food for her husband.

(pages 52 & 53)

2 Pictures **a** & **c**

3 b; **c**; **e**; **g**; **h**

4 a too much **b** too many **c** too much **d** too many ... enough
e More **f** more **g** Too many **h** more

FRIENDSHIP

(pages 54 & 55)

2 a Suzie Orr – tries to put the right students together
b Jean Norris – ended up working with her roommate
c Julie Noel – didn't like her shy roommate

3 a Julie Noel and her Roommate – sad
b Alan Sussman and his Roommate – happy
c Jean Norris and Renee Neufville – happy

4 b I wish I had asked her about her problems.
c I wish her other friends had wanted me in their group.
d I wish they hadn't said horrible things about me.
e I wish I hadn't forgotten her birthday.
f I wish I had been strong enough to keep our friendship going.

(pages 56 & 57)

2 a-J; b-L; c-B; d-J; e-L

3 1 Girls are closer to each other; they tell their secrets and discuss feelings.
2 Girls' friendships last longer than boys' friendships.

4 1 "I mean, it's much more important for girls, having close friends."
2 "I don't think that's a specially good thing, keeping the same friends for ever."

5 b It is very important, keeping in touch with your friends.
c It often helps people, just listening to their problems.
d It upsets me, thinking about the fights I have had with friends.
e It is a sign of real friendship, being ready to help.

GREEN ISSUES

(pages 58 & 59)

2 b; c; d; g; h; i

3 1 smog air pollution
2 traffic jams, congestion
3 the greenhouse effect, greenhouse gases

4 a-4; b-2; c-5; d-1; e-6; f-3

(pages 60 & 61)

2 a-T; b-F; c-F; d-T; e-F; f -T; g-F

3 • beauty for visitors
• danger of climate change
• important for medical science

4 We have to save them; otherwise there will be a catastrophic change in the whole world's climate.

5 a We must change our attitude. Otherwise there will be an ecological disaster.
b We must save these animals. Otherwise our grandchildren will blame us.
c We must use energy more carefully, or pollution will continue to increase.
d We must respect the Earth. Otherwise it will die.
e We must think about the future. Otherwise we won't have one.

9 The point which goes with the picture:
• destruction of the countryside

HONESTY

(pages 62 & 63)

2 a Eighty wallets containing £30 were left lying around in different places around Britain.
b Men
c Because he thought it might have sentimental value.
d He was unemployed and he thought the person who had lost it might also be unemployed.

3 a If a shop assistant gave you too much change by mistake, what would you do?
b If you saw someone cheating in an exam, would you report them?
c If you crashed your motorbike into an expensive car and nobody saw you, would you tell the police?
d If your rich friend forgot he had lent you £20, would you remind him?
e How would you feel if you lost your wallet containing £50?
f Would you tell the waiter if he forgot to charge you for your drink?

(pages 64 & 65)

2 b-S; d (Michael talks about it but hasn't done it); f-M; g-M; h-L

Key Language
Michael – "I lied about my age. But I don't think it's wrong in that situation." **Louise** – "I totally disapprove of people who don't pay the proper fare." **Sylvia** – "I'm scared of getting caught. But I don't think it's immoral."

LANGUAGE

(pages 66 & 67)

2 The only suitable title would be **a**.

3 a-F; b-T; c-F; d-F; e-T; f-F; g-T

4 a a film star b a bird's nest c a private cinema d cat food
e a computer f being in prison

(pages 68 & 69)

2 a Bina b Dinesh ... Bina c Bina d Dinesh e Bina f Bina

3 Because her grandmother doesn't speak English.

4 Because all the words connected to the wedding are in Hindi. In many cases, there may not be an English word.

5 Bina says: "People throw in English words all the time – words and phrases and sometimes whole sentences."

6 a weather b depends c It d teacher e time f depending

9 a+2; b+4; c+9; d+1; e+5; f+10; g+8; h+3; i+11; j+6; k+12; l+7

10 My friend can be really stupid sometimes. He stopped to get some cigarettes and left the car open. He talked to the girl in the shop for about five minutes, and some man stole his stereo and two hundred pounds from the car. Then he called the police – but what can they do?

NEW TECHNOLOGY

(pages 70 & 71)

2 a-F; b-T; c-T; d-F; e-T; f-F

3 Few students believe the Internet is dangerous so most are happy with it.
Some university lecturers and psychologists think it may cause problems.

4 a surfing b modern c online d download e virtual

(pages 72 & 73)

2 The two examples shown in the photos are CD-ROMs and computer-controlled robots in industry. The other uses which she mentions are computer systems in supermarkets and word-processing.

3 a "... computer systems in supermarkets – they make the whole operation quicker and cheaper; it's easier for the shop and for the customer."
b "They are more accurate ... than human workers... "
c "Today we are only at the very beginning. Just imagine what computers will be able to do in a hundred years from now."
d "They are ... cheaper than human workers... "
e "... it's easier to find things on a CD-ROM."
f "... we use less paper, and we send fewer documents by post."

4 Look at... ; Think about... ; Take for example... ; Another example is...

6 "Santa" means "Santa Claus" – another name for Father Christmas.

POVERTY

(pages 74 & 75)

2 Here it means "sleeping on the streets".

3 Yes, it is true – the figure is 700,000.

4 critics-F; the Austin city council-A; the general public-A; Peggy Wilson-A; the group that feeds people-F; the Downtown Austin Alliance-A; the homeless task force-F; Tom Hatch-F

5 hardheartedness; (*paragraph 2*)

6 **b** helplessness **c** meanness **d** tiredness **e** poverty **f** kindness **g** lateness

(pages 76 & 77)

2 $50 – "But what can you get if you sell your old TV – $50?"/ "But just think what $50 could do for people in, say, Ethiopia."
12 million – "Around the world over 12 million young children die every year – mostly because their parents are too poor to get basic food and medicines.
20% – "... 20% of American children live in poverty... "
15 cents – "the [measles] vaccine ... costs 15 cents
one million – "More than one million [young children] die of measles... "

3 American children do not die of measles because they are vaccinated.

4 (*Suggested answer*) Emily thinks that we should deal with the problem of poverty in America first – before thinking about Africa.

5 a; c; e

RACISM

(pages 78 & 79)

2 e; c; a; b; d; f; h; g

3 The suitable title is **b**

4 Dressed in smart casual clothes Mr Leary, **39**, waited for about 20 minutes.

5 **b** George Bush, the ex-president of the USA, is coming to speak at the conference next week.
c Ms Santoni, 23, is a candidate in the general election.
d Hong Kong, once a British colony, is now a city in China.
e Soccer, now the most popular international sport in the world, started in England almost 200 years ago.
f Bill Gates, the richest man in the world, started his career as a software writer.
g The *Mona Lisa* ("*La Gioconda*"), painted by Leonardo da Vinci, is now in the Louvre in Paris.

(pages 80 & 81)

2 Tarik

3 They really meant "Don't marry that man."

4 a-F; b-F; c-T; d-T; e-F; f-T

5 "What changed their attitudes was our children."

6 **b** What I really hate is hypocrisy.
c What is very important is the attitude of your neighbours.
d What changed their views was love for their grandchildren.
e What makes life difficult in some parts of London is racism.
f What separates a lot of couples is pressure from the family.

REBELLION

(pages 82 & 83)

2 b-1; c-2; e-3; h-4; g-5; a-6; f-7; d-8; i-9

3 **b** Kate's mother wouldn't give her money to get her ears pierced.
c She won't conform.
d She wouldn't give her more than one month's rent.
e Many teenagers walk out because their parents won't listen to them.
f Why won't he think about the future?

4 **a** get out **b** hang out **c** move out of **d** walk out **e** throw ... out

5 Personal pronouns are left out, eg. "Cries, threatens, bangs on my bedroom door". "Personal pronoun "She" is omitted. Possessive adjectives are left out, eg. "Kate demands money for getting ears pierced." Possessive adjective "her" is omitted. Direct speech is used without introductory verb or speech marks – italics are used instead, eg. "Volunteers phone number – *just don't think you can ring me all the time*." A fuller version would be "She volunteers her phone number. Then she says, *"Just don't think you can ring me all the time.*" Other features of the diary style are the omission of articles, eg. "Watching her stuff clothes in [a] bag... ", "Search [the] area where I know she hangs out" and the use of the present tense.

(pages 84 & 85)

got divorced   drugs   school   came out   success   mixture
got together   was born   *Insecticide*   shot himself

3 **a**-7: drop out of   **b**-1: come out   **c**-3: smash up
d-2: get together with   **e**-8: get off   **f**-5: bring out
g-9: give up   **h**-6: burn out   **i**-4: fade away

SEXISM

(pages 86 & 87)

2 **a** – Because no one ever thinks of calling the father when a child is ill.
b – Because some female high achievers, such as Margaret Thatcher, often don't promote other women.
c – Because women say sorry, sorry, sorry all the time.
d – Because women are told to start out as secretaries, and good secretaries rarely get promoted.
e – Because women are either too tough or not tough enough.
f – Because a woman is still judged on her looks.
g – Because men think women won't be as committed to their job once they have a child.

3 is ... judged;   are told ... get promoted;   are made

4 **b** Women are expected to do the housework.
c Women and men are judged by different standards.
d Women are promoted much more quickly.
e Powerful women are feared and distrusted.
f The best jobs are often kept for men.
g More time is given to boys in the classroom./Boys are given more time in the classroom.

5 (*Some suggestions*)
Why Women Don't Get To The Top
It's Hard To Get To The Top – For Women
19 Reasons Why Women Aren't Bosses

6 **Men's Attitudes:**
Because men think women won't be as committed to their job once they have a child.
Because "women get all moody and useless once a month."
Because a woman is still judged on her looks.

Because working mothers are made to feel guilty.
Because women are either too tough or not tough enough.
Because "women's brains are smaller."
Because men fear and distrust powerful women.
Because a lot of men genuinely think of themselves as superior to women.

Childcare and Housework:
Because women have babies.
Because men think women won't be as committed to their job once they have a child.
Because women are busy doing housework when they could be training, impressing the boss and networking.
Because working mothers are made to feel guilty.
Because no one ever thinks of calling the father when a child is ill.

(pages 88 & 89)

3

	Sandra	her brothers
gifts	Barbie dolls	doctor sets
extra lessons	piano lessons	*math tuition*
activities with parents	washing-up	baseball
parents' ambitions for them	marry a doctor	be doctors

5 b-6; c-4; d-3; e-2; f-1

6 a support b housewife c equal opportunities d stereotyping e ambitions

9 Men's sports – football; baseball; boxing; motor-racing; rugby; sumo-wrestling

SPORT

(pages 90 & 91)

2 a 19 million b 84 c 16 d 28,000 ... 500 (one quarter of 2000) e 240 million

3 b-1; c-3; d-7; e-2; f-5; g-4

4 The article aims to make lazy people feel good about themselves. It is talking to unsporty, inactive people, not sporty people. It is unlikely to make anyone who is interested in sport give it up.

(pages 92 & 93)

2 b; d; e; g

3 a professional football players b them ... most

Key Language
Some other verbs taking two objects are: "hand", "pass", "write", read".

4 a that joke b to everyone c the police d to everyone f some money g to everyone

Advertising
PAGE 3

2
- a You *can't* still be in the bath.
- b I'm meeting Sally today. It's been ten years since we last met, so she *might not* recognise me!
- c Correct
- d Correct
- e Correct
- f She *can't* be your mother, she looks far too young!
- g I *might* arrive tomorrow, or maybe on Wednesday, it all depends on the children.

Animal rights
PAGE 4

1
- a iv – after a preposition
- b vi – after a preposition
- c i – as a noun
- d ii – verb is subject of sentence
- e iii – after verb *hate*
- f vii – verb is subject of sentence
- g v – verb is subject of sentence

3

G	E	N	E	T	I	C	U	P	G
E	X	T	I	N	C	T	I	O	N
N	I	R	N	P	I	Y	R	A	I
E	L	A	S	I	R	X	A	C	T
S	L	P	K	U	C	R	B	H	N
M	P	C	E	F	U	O	B	E	U
O	T	M	O	U	S	E	I	R	H
A	C	T	I	V	I	S	T	N	O

- a extinction
- b activist
- c circus
- d genes
- e poacher
- f trap
- g rabbit
- h mouse
- i genetic
- j hunting

Art and artists
PAGE 5

1
- a earn – I work so hard and only *earn* £200 a week!
- b become – As I *become* older, I find it harder to hear people.
- c receive – She never *received* my letter!
- d understand – That film was so complicated, I didn't *understand* it at all!
- e travel – How did you *travel* to Thailand?
- f arrive – I *arrived* at work half an hour late yesterday!
- g hurt – It *hurts* me to see you so upset.

2
- a v – climb out of bed
- b i – have a good relationship
- c vi – finish
- d iii – make contact
- e vii – survive
- f ii – attack
- g iv – travel around

3
- a get
- b get by
- c get
- d get about
- e get up
- f get
- g getting at
- h get through
- i getting

Beauty
PAGE 6

1

VERB	AFFIRMATIVE	NEGATIVE	QUESTION
to go	used to go	didn't use to go	did you use to go?
to wear	used to wear	didn't use to wear	did you use to wear?
to fly	used to fly	didn't use to fly	did you use to fly?
to visit	used to visit	didn't use to visit	did you use to visit?

2
- a started
- b used to appear
- c used to fly
- d went
- e used to call
- f used to love, became
- g used to love

Beliefs
PAGE 7

1
- a I *do* own this car!
- b Ian *does* speak French!
- c I *did* phone you last night!
- d I *do* have some money!
- e Charlie *did* tell me!
- f Jane *does* work with me!
- g He *did* get the letter!

2
- 1a I don't speak French but I *do speak* German.
- 1b I used to live in Berlin, so I *speak* German.
- 2a I hate cabbage but I *do like* lettuce.
- 2b I quite like cabbage and I *like* lettuce.
- 3a I felt better when he *apologised*.
- 3b I was so angry with him but he *did apologise*.
- 4a "I don't think you went to work today!" "I *did go* to work. Ask my boss!"
- 4b "Where were you today?" "I *went* to work. Ask my boss!"

Crime and punishment
PAGE 8

1
- a Q
- b R
- c R
- d Q
- e Q
- f Q
- g R
- h R

2
- a You don't come from here, *do you*?
- b I gave it to you, *didn't I*?
- c Russia's the world's biggest country, *isn't it*?
- d You wouldn't lie to me, *would you*?
- e Sally's got flu, *hasn't she*?
- f The Pottens have gone on holiday, *haven't they*?
- g You will phone me when you get there, *won't you*?

Discipline

1
a Pupils under the age of 16 *are not allowed* to smoke. Smoking *is banned* from the corridors and classrooms.
b Alcohol *is banned* from all school premises.
c The teachers *don't like* students arriving late, and sometimes fine them.
d Lessons *are supposed* to start at 9.30 but often start a few minutes late.
e Although the teachers *are supposed to* look smart, students *are allowed to* wear whatever they like.
f Language students *are not supposed* to speak any language except English, but it is very difficult when there are so many people from the same country.
g Cheating in tests *is banned*, and anyone caught cheating is sent home.

Drink and drugs

1
a saw
b started
c had moved
d haven't had
e was
f had arrived
g haven't seen

2
a I've lived in this house ten years.
b Correct
c I moved house in 1976 and I *have lived* there ever since.
d Correct
e Correct
f Correct
g By dinner time, Lucy *had* already *eaten* all her chocolates!

Family

1
a "I want my freedom back."
b "I've fallen in love with another woman."
c "My parents are putting pressure on me to get married."
d "I don't want to grow old alone."
e "I'm thinking of leaving Tim."
f "I'll miss my children if I leave."
g "It's difficult having a family and a career."

2
a Jack confessed he'd said some terrible things to his wife.
b Thomas felt arranged marriages were a good idea.
c Alice thought fewer people would get married in the future.
d Ian admitted he had had an affair.
e Jo announced she was getting a divorce.
f Sally explained she couldn't stop them being together.
g Bob agreed they should get married.

Fashion

ADJECTIVE	COMPARATIVE
young	younger
late	later
fat	fatter
heavy	heavier
intelligent	more intelligent
good	better
bad	worse

1
a thinner
b prettier
c taller
d worse
e wider
f slimmer
g more attractive
h more artistic

2
a It's so tiring having children. I *feel* 10 years older.
b I can see you've lost weight – you look *healthier* now.
c "How are you today?" "Not that good doctor. In fact, I feel a lot *worse* than I did yesterday."
d Oh yes, darling, I like it! You *look* so much better with short hair!
e You sound *younger* on the phone.
f This bag is almost empty – that's why it feels *lighter* than yours.
g Listen to this tape – it *sounds* much clearer than the other one.

Film and TV

1
a She's being asked for her name.
b The room was being painted yesterday.
c My jeans are being washed.
d The chairs were being moved into the lecture hall.
e The man was being questioned about the robbery.
f John's being taught at home.
g Mary was being watched all the time.

2
a These days, films are more *violent* than they were in the past.
b There was a story in the newspaper about a *murder* in which a woman was stabbed to death.
c People who get pleasure from killing are *sadistic*.
d I think it's *terrible* that there is so much violence in children's computer games.
e In America, there is a lot of violence because possession of *guns* is legal.
f A *copycat* killing is one which is identical to another killing.
g Murder and theft are examples of *crimes*.

3
I see the *terrible* images
They show upon my screen,
Of another sadistic *murder*
And I wonder what they mean.
If we see a *copycat* killing
Out upon the street,
Will the media apologise
For creating this *violent* repeat?

Food

1
a "£10 per ticket? I only have £5! I *don't have enough* money!"
b Well, we've got 6 loaves, plenty of cheese and lots of fruit. There should be *enough* for everyone.
c There's *too much* bad news in the newspapers these days!
d We were late but we had *enough* time to get to the airport.
e London's so polluted – there are *too many* cars on the roads.
f Ten kids... eight tickets... Oh! I *don't have enough* tickets!
g Don't eat *too much* junk food – it's very bad for you!

2
  a ANOREXIA
  b SLAUGHTERHOUSES
  c STAPLES
  d VEGGIE
  e JUNK FOOD
  f FACTORY
  g PEANUT BUTTER

3 Possible answers:
  a Too much money is spent on advertising fast food. Not enough money is spent on advertising healthy eating.
  b People don't eat enough fruit. They eat too much meat.
  c Too many people eat at fast food restaurants. Not enough people go to health food shops.
  d Enough information on healthy eating is available. Not enough people use it.

Friendship

1
  a I wish I had more time with my family.
  b I wish I hadn't argued with my grandfather on the day he died.
  c I wish I hadn't split up with my first wife.
  d I wish I could write good songs.
  e I wish I had learnt a musical instrument when I was young.
  f I wish I hadn't left school without any qualifications.
  g I wish I didn't smoke 40 cigarettes a day.
  h I wish I hadn't taken drugs when I was younger.

3
  a iii – self-confident
  b v – thoughtful
  c i – proud
  d iv – generous
  e vi – retiring
  f ii – modest
  g viii – cautious
  h vii – liberal

Green issues

PAGE 16

1
  a needed
  b been
  c chosen
  d stopped
  e brought
  f waited
  g liked
  h become

2 has decreased, have, use, has also changed, are, have gone down, have risen, faces

H	U	D	N	J	R	O	R	P	F	A	M
A	P	G	R	I	E	C	V	B	A	S	P
X	O	K	U	E	S	S	L	N	C	W	Y
I	L	J	R	S	O	N	R	L	I	B	F
C	L	U	A	T	U	J	M	R	D	Y	U
F	U	E	L	B	R	H	O	V	R	Z	M
B	T	A	K	D	C	L	I	M	A	T	E
G	I	C	M	W	E	O	T	P	I	X	S
C	O	N	G	E	S	T	I	O	N	Z	B
A	N	H	T	K	P	O	C	F	W	N	A

3 Honesty

PAGE 17

1
  a If I went to London I'd visit the Millennium Dome.
  b I would feel guilty if I cheated in an exam.
  c I would be an actor if I could change my job.
  d I'd live in Paris if I spoke French.
  e If I found a wallet on the street I would take it to the police.
  f If I were a successful pop star I would wear outrageous clothes.
  g If I could buy a car I would choose a BMW.
  h If I had a better camera I'd take better pictures.

Language

PAGE 18

1
  a Verb
  b Adverb
  c Adverb
  d Verb
  e Adverb
  f Adverb
  g Verb

3
  a telly
  b thick
  c nick
  d guy
  e booze
  f lingo (slang for "language")

New technology

PAGE 19

1 Look at... Think about... Take for example... And what about...? Then there's... Another example is...

2 Modern medicine is wonderful. *Think about* the things they can do nowadays. *Take for example* transplants – if your heart is diseased they can change it for a healthy one. *And what about* fertility? So many more couples are being helped to have children. *Then there's* giving birth itself – so much safer and less painful than before. And *look at* the drugs we have now, which have helped to destroy diseases like smallpox. *Another example is* AZT, which helps to control AIDS.

Anagram = virtual

Poverty

PAGE 20

1
  a shyness
  b timidity
  c anger
  d weakness
  e happiness
  f confidence
  g thirst
  h tiredness

2
a   To prevent the problem of *lateness* we do not allow people into the theatre after the play has started.
b   Thanks to the *carelessness* of the burglars, it was easy for the police to catch them.
c   The townspeople felt a lot of *anger* that nothing was being done about homelessness.
d   My idea of *happiness* is a hot bath, a good book, and a box of chocolates. There's nothing better!
e   It's time for the rich countries to do their bit to fight *poverty*.
f   Some people think animals are naturally kind, but there's a lot of *cruelty* in nature.
g   To do a job, you must be sure you can do it – *confidence* in yourself is very important!

Racism

1
What made him late was a flat tyre.
What I love most about Italy are the delicious pasta dishes.
What she was looking for in the library were books on American history.
What I really enjoyed in the film was the beautiful photography.
What makes life difficult for some women is combining a career and a family.
What they went on holiday for was the sunshine.
What I'm hoping to buy in the sales are some cheap shoes.
What we really need is racial equality and justice for all.

2   Possible answers:
a   What I like about my country is the weather.
b   What I hate about studying English is the grammar.
c   What annoyed me this morning was the traffic.
d   What makes me laugh are my wife's jokes.
e   What I look for in a boy/girlfriend is a sense of humour.
f   What I wanted for my birthday was a new computer.
g   What I enjoy doing at the weekend is going out dancing.
h   What I detest about computers is staring at the screen.

3
a   v – dislike of others because of the colour of his/her skin
b   vi – people linked by a common race or culture
c   ii – to fit in with society
d   i – the old political system of South Africa where people were treated differently according to race
e   viii – the police identification for a black person
f   iii – policy which favours someone because of his/her race
g   iv – a right-wing racist political party in Britain
h   vii – a marriage between people of different races

Rebellion

1
a   R   He will spend all evening on his computer.
b   A   He would never cook a meal.
c   A   He would take the bus everywhere.
d   R   He won't wear anything that isn't in fashion.
e   A   He wouldn't let his children use bad language in the house.
f   R   He will spend hours in the bathroom.
g   A   He would sit in that chair and smoke his pipe in the evenings.

Sexism

1
a   Ben and Zoe love Coca-Cola. They drink far too much of it. (active)
b   Coca-Cola is the world's most popular drink. It's drunk everywhere. (passive)
c   Canada has two languages. English and French are spoken there. (passive)
d   Sam's an expert at languages. She speaks English and French. (active)
e   Lotus makes great cars. It makes them in the UK. (active)
f   Minis are great cars. They're made in the UK. (passive)

2
a   make
b   are seen
c   is praised
d   praise
e   are told
f   do
g   are not taught
h   are ignored

Sport

2
a   Sponsor gives swimming club £10,000.
b   Leeds pays Greek football club £5 million for player.
c   Athlete tells Olympic Committee the truth about drug-taking.
d   Juventus player shown red card for foul.
e   Company gives new equipment to hockey team.
f   Club gives prize to best athlete.
g   Doctor refuses athlete permission to run.

3
a   boxing
b   tennis
c   rugby
d   showjumping
e   swimming
f   skiing
g   basketball